Bitch Incorporated

How to Bitch Appropriately Without Being Bitchy

For Men and Women

by
Samantha Payne Ph.D.

authorHOUSE™

1663 LIBERTY DRIVE, SUITE 200
BLOOMINGTON, INDIANA 47403
(800) 839-8640
WWW.AUTHORHOUSE.COM

First published by AuthorHouse 07/13/05

ISBN: 1-4208-4379-6 (sc)

Printed in the United States of America
Bloomington, Indiana

This book is printed on acid-free paper.

To Dan - my husband, soul mate, best friend,
and muse who is always there for me
To Jessica - whose love for and belief in me
forced me to complete this book
To Marla - who overcame shyness to draw the
pictures

And finally, in Memory of Russell
Your short life, and the lessons you taught, are
not forgotten.

Table of Contents

Introduction

I believe I must have been born this way. Could I have known as I slid forth into this world that the doctor was botching my birth and nearly killing my mother? If so, how difficult, how incredibly frustrating it must have been for I did not yet have command of the words with which to confront him. Without words, we can choose only screams or silence. I'm sure I screamed. Can it be that my assertive personality was determined in those first few moments?

My mother often stated that I was the only one of her four daughters who brought home stray people rather than stray animals. My "collection of" and concern for people allowed me to observe large cross sections of humanity and sealed my fate as a crusader. For a while I clung to the belief that all people are born with the courage, determination, knowledge and necessary tools to stand up for themselves. How naïve I was.

Eventually I was able to separate desire from fact and admit that huge numbers of both adults and kids allow other people to walk all over them. The results are devastating. People who do not stand up for themselves are constantly irritated, angry, sad, and/or fearful. They lack self respect. Sometimes they take their hurt and anger out on others; just as often they punish themselves.

By the time I was in my late teens, I was seriously considering opening a business called BITCH INCORPORATED. I hated to see those I cared about taken advantage of. I hated to see folks I did not even know taken advantage of. Heck, I even hated to see people I didn't particularly like taken advantage of. I reasoned that, rather than allow injustice to continue, rather than have the little person, the good person, the honest person, the innocent person lose, I would hire myself out and do their bitching for them. I loved the idea; people I talked with over the next few years loved the idea. Sadly, it was not to be. In order to have a baby (a long story I will not relate here), I became a psychologist.

As a psychologist, I was able to help people learn (for a much higher fee, of course) when, how, why and where to assert themselves. Yet the lure of a business called BITCH INCORPORATED roamed restlessly through the pathways of my mind. Ultimately I had to face the fact that far more people could benefit from a book than from any kind of one-on-one service I could provide -- whether as a psychologist or as the sole staff member of BITCH INCORPORATED. I must admit, the idea of writing a book was not half as appealing as actively doing other people's bitching for them, but....

So here it is. I hope you will enjoy the read. My goal has been to make the information helpful but not heavy, the reading fun as well as informative, to bring a smile to your face and laughter to your lips, courage to your actions and peace to your soul.

Is This Book for You?

Take this simple test:

Do I shy away from confrontation?

Do I fear standing up for myself?

Do I make excuses to avoid standing up for myself?

Do I allow others to take advantage of me?

Do I get down on myself because I let others run my life?

Do I yearn to stand up for myself in ways I can be proud of?

Do I worry too much about what other people think of me?

Do I become angry but seldom resolve the situation that is upsetting me?

Do I feel dissatisfied with the way I stand up for myself?

If you have answered any of these questions with a yes, this book is definitely for you. BUY THIS BOOK!

The Commitment

Are you willing to allow change to occur? Are you willing to read, think a bit and cooperate when your mind suggests trying something different? Would you like to move from merely complaining to complaining in a way that will make a difference? If the answer is no, DO NOT BUY THIS BOOK. Put it down, put it down right now and walk away. If you have already purchased this book, return it to the store, immediately! With luck they will give you a refund. If they refuse, give this book to a friend. (I'm sure your friend will have received far worse gifts.) However, if you are willing to allow change to occur, KEEP THIS BOOK AND KEEP ON READING. Soon you should find yourself responding like this early reader of BITCH INCORPORATED.

"My husband and I were driving from St. Louis to Maine and stopped for the night at a hotel. The next morning I got into the elevator with 5 teenage girls and their soccer coach to go down to the lobby for the continental breakfast while my husband was showering. Our plan was to have a quick breakfast so we could get an early start. However, for no apparent reason the elevator got stuck. We pushed the alarm button and sounded the alarm but nothing happened. After waiting a little we picked up the emergency phone and were connected to the front desk. The clerk said the system would be reset but still nothing happened.

We were feeling hot and cramped. We called again, but the clerk wasn't particularly forthcoming about a plan to rescue us. Finally, using the coach's cell phone, we called a parent of one of the girls who was visibly upset at being confined. The parent went to the front desk and said he'd call 911 if the clerk wouldn't. After an hour of standing in this hot little elevator, we were finally freed by the fire department. I was too hot, tired and upset to eat and might have simply paid our bill and left, but I had just read BITCH INC. So, I decided to screw up my courage, tell the desk clerk how unhappy I was about spending that hour stuck in that hot elevator with very little communication from them. The hotel advertised their 100% satisfactory guarantee and I definitely was not satisfied. The clerk offered a mere 10% reduction to our bill which did not seem fair. Encouraged to take a stand by what I had read in your book, I asked to talk to the manager. Because the manager wasn't on site, I had to call back the next day. The little vignettes in the book encouraged me to follow through. The result was a polite, pleasant conversation followed by a complete refund! BITCH INCORPORATE paid for itself many times over with this one incident. Thank you. The Johnsons"

Learn This Rule

IF SOMETHING IS BOTHERING YOU, ADDRESS IT!

If something is bothering you, no matter how trivial it seems, address it!

If something is bothering you, no matter how scary it feels, address it!

If something is bothering you, no matter how busy you are, address it!

IF SOMETHING IS BOTHERING YOU, ADDRESS IT!

Beyond Commitment

Once you have made the commitment to address an issue, your attention can shift. You are now ready to decide the *best way* to address this particular issue.

Deciding the best way to address a particular issue is where your energy rightfully belongs. You will no longer waste valuable energy avoiding confrontation or trying to convince yourself whatever is bothering you doesn't really matter, or that it will blow over, or that you don't have the power to make a difference, or that your feelings are not *that* important. Just as relevant, you will no longer waste time playing the incident over and over in your mind, stirring up all those negative feelings and dragging yourself ever downward. Why? Because you will no longer have time to waste. You will be far too busy developing your plan. Your time and energy are needed and now will be utilized in taking new, positive and (my favorite) creative steps.

Feeling Good About You

Do you know the most common reason people give for not standing up for themselves? They worry about what other people will think of them. They fail to understand that the real danger lurks not so much in what others think but in losing sight of who they are. Here is an analogy. (Of course, when our daughter first heard this she just rolled her eyes and said, "Mom, all your analogies have to do with food." Ok, I'm guilty, she's right! But, what's wrong with food?)

Let's imagine that your best friend came to you one day and told you that she had just learned, from a completely reliable contact, that every source of food had been contaminated.

Let's pretend this same friend tells you that she can get you enough frosting or cake (yes, I said **or**) to last until the contamination is dealt with. Yup, you have to choose between the frosting and the cake; you can't have both.

Which would you choose? Even sweets-lover that I am, I would choose the cake (albeit very reluctantly) since cake has some nutritional value in the form of eggs, milk and flour. It therefore offers the possibility of sustaining life. Frosting has no nutritional value. It is very tasty, but it's all fluff.

Think about this. Let's have the cake represent how we feel about ourselves and the frosting represent how others feel about us. If we feel good about ourselves, we can survive even if others don't like us. However, if others feel good about us, but we don't feel good about ourselves, we will simply dismiss their opinions concluding, "They simply do not know the real me." Thus we end up feeling worse than ever about ourselves. Most of us WANT the approval of others but please listen up -- we DO NOT NEED the approval of others. We honestly can survive without their approval. What we DO NEED is self respect. We cannot survive long or well without it.

Happily there are many times when we can have both the cake and the frosting. There are times when we stand up for our beliefs and others agree with us and/or respect us for our actions. I will be the first to admit, it is great to have both. Obviously this does not happen all the time. If we become too focused on securing the approval of others, we will likely forget to stand up appropriately for ourselves. We need to remember that cake and frosting are wonderful together and preferred by the majority of us sweets lovers. However, when we can't have both we must learn to choose the cake. Frosting alone will never sustain us. This surely gives new meaning to the old saying, "That's the frosting on the cake!" Our goal then is to find appropriate ways to act that lead to feeling good about ourselves.

LESSON ONE:
To Bitch or Not To Bitch, That is the Question

This question is not an easy one for most people to answer. Too many people tend to equate bitching with being a bitch. They label the act of lodging a complaint as somehow bad, out of line, inappropriate, uncalled for, or obnoxious. They don't want to draw attention to themselves or risk making others uncomfortable. They don't want to upset others or risk not being liked. Heaven forbid that we should make waves, confront people with their behavior or expect them to be responsible for their actions! And we wonder what is wrong with today's world!

The fact is if we don't learn to speak up, to stand up for our rights, to express our needs, to let others know we will not be taken advantage of, then we are sending people the message that what they are doing is okay with us. It is okay for a manufacturer to produce inferior products and sell them to us. It is okay for a service provider to engage in shoddy practice or workmanship. It is okay to be lied to, cheated, taken advantage of by companies, acquaintances, friends, co-workers, and even family members. If all this is true, it then follows that it is okay for all of us to refuse to accept responsibility for our own actions, right? WRONG!

The fact of standing up for ourselves does not make us bitches nor does it indicate we are bitchy. Ultimately, the way we choose to stand up for ourselves will define us much more accurately and completely than the *fact* of standing up for ourselves. For a marriage, family, friendship, group, business, company, town, state, country to run smoothly, caring confrontation utilizing clear communication is a must. So let's get going and learn to bitch appropriately. We can bitch (verb) without being a bitch (noun). In other words, we can bitch without being bitchy.

LESSON TWO:
Win Some, Lose Some

Do not set yourself up. Consider this fact: neither you, nor I, nor anyone else can always win. You will not win every confrontation. Whether you win or lose you must learn to respect yourself for the *fact* that you stood up for your values and for the *way* that you conducted yourself. With time and practice you will get better at standing up for your beliefs. You will develop more confidence as you increase your skills. As a result you will undoubtedly win more battles. However, no matter how good you get, I can promise you there will still be battles that you will lose. Pride in and respect for self must come from your willingness to stand up for what you believe is right. You should not and must not beat up on yourself when you lose. Standing up for yourself and your beliefs in an appropriate fashion will result in gaining and retaining your self-respect.

I remember very clearly my first big loss. As a high school senior, I was editor of my class yearbook. A year earlier a classmate of ours, albeit not one of the in crowd, committed suicide. This young man was very intelligent -- and very silent. He seldom communicated with others. It was said, although his father had an excellent job, that he and his family lived up on the mountain in a shack. I worried about Russell. His clothes didn't fit; often his body and clothes were noticeably dirty. He smelled bad. While a few would make comments, most were silent. Perhaps cruelest of all however, Russell was not a meaningful part of our world.

I remember in grade school sending Russell many Valentines so his Valentine box would not be empty. I'm sure there were others who made similarly infrequent gestures of concern through the years. We didn't mean to be dismissive. But, we had our own lives.

When Russell killed himself, I was convinced that we, Russell's classmates, had not contributed positively to his life. Perhaps this was easier than wondering if we had contributed to his death. We had never given him the gift of solid friendship, never offered him a listening ear, and never forced ourselves through his shell of silence. I was determined that, in death at least, Russell would have the recognition he never had in life. I wanted to dedicate our yearbook to him rather than follow the traditional path by dedicating it to a teacher. I wanted a full-page picture of Russell with a black border; I wanted the words "In Memoriam." I wanted each and every one of us, teachers, students and principals alike, to remember --and to learn. I fought and I fought and I lost.   The administration nixed the idea. "Not appropriate," they said.   Losing that battle bothers me to this day (thus the dedication of this book), but I have never regretted making the attempt.

LESSON THREE:
Ask and Ye <u>Might</u> Receive

There are many wonderful people and companies out there who not only are willing but committed to standing behind their actions, words and/or products. They are proud of their products and take pride in themselves. However, they cannot correct wrongs if they do not know about them. It is our job as consumers to provide feedback.

I remember one Christmas I opened a box of Sees chocolates only to find they were stale. Rather than becoming upset, sad, or angry (no easy task for a chocoholic), rather than throwing the chocolates away and forgetting about them (perish the thought), or accepting the stale chocolates as an act of fate (or as a warning from the calorie and cholesterol gods), I called Sees. Their customer service number is readily available on the packaging of their product. The representative who answered my call could not have been nicer. She wrote down the required information and within a short period of time, I had received a letter of apology and a replacement box of candy.

I remember the morning my husband's Sonicare toothbrush stopped holding a charge. Dan had purchased this toothbrush four years earlier and assumed he would have to buy a new one. However, before making this purchase, Dan decided to call Sonicare. The representative told him they would happily replace his toothbrush with a new one for $50 (thirty-five dollars less than the best price we had found). Sonicare paid for the postage and for the return of the old toothbrush.

Then there was the time we received an assortment of goodies from my step-daughter, Tonia, via Figis mail-order company. We had received Figis products in the past and had always been impressed with the quality and satisfied with the amount. However, this time the product was not up to its usual standards, and we wrote to the company explaining the problem. Tonia's money was refunded immediately with an apology to both of us.

ReSound, the company who manufactured my husband's first hearing aids, provides another tremendous example of fairness. Dan was part of the initial test group. Not only was Dan able to buy his hearing aids at a discount but, although this was not part of the deal, the company maintained the aids free of charge for several years. When ReSound recently came out with a new, improved hearing aid, Dan was among one of the first to buy it. Dan has been and continues to be a great ambassador for this company and product.

Are you beginning to understand why I keep repeating, IT NEVER HURTS TO ASK? Do you need more convincing? Okay, here are some more examples.

When we broke the lock-in mechanism on the mixing bowl of our food processor, Cusinart replaced it for free, even though it was no longer covered by a warranty; when the gasket on the blender went bad, this also was replaced free of charge. In both cases Cusinart paid the postage.

In similar fashion, Moen replaced two 5-year-old faucet parts free of any kind of charge.

My sister, Moreen, was going through a difficult period in her life. She inadvertently bounced a check, and the bank charged her $26 service fee. Rather than becoming angry or mentally beating up on herself, Moreen called the bank, reminded them she had been an excellent customer for thirty years, and asked them to remove the service charge. They did.

We doubted the company would do anything about it when our Fisher/Paykel dishwasher started to slough off small pieces of rust. After all, we had purchased the dishwasher three years earlier. However, following our own rule, Dan and I decided to call the company. Yes, we reminded ourselves, IT NEVER HURTS TO ASK! What concerned, caring people we talked to. The Fisher/Paykel representatives immediately determined that a steel bar across top of the dish washer was the culprit. This part should have been specially treated to prevent rusting, they declared, and immediately shipped us their brand new dishwasher model. This marvelous company even arranged and paid for the installation.

Hewlett-Packard was equally incredible when our 11.5 month old four-in-one copier/fax/scanner/printer stopped working. They shipped a new one to us immediately by Fed Ex and we were up and running again within five days.

HP paid shipping for the new machine and for return of the old one. Shall I say it one more time? IT NEVER HURTS TO ASK!

Of course, it is not always this easy. Not all companies stand behind their products. It is equally true that some companies will give you the run-around before agreeing to take action. I remember when, paying a large credit card bill of well over one thousand dollars, I goofed. I had recorded the amount correctly in my check book but reversed two numbers when writing the check. This resulted in a $60 credit card balance. The credit card company charged me interest not only on the $60 balance but on the entire amount. When I questioned this action, I was told by the company representative that this was company policy. Totally frustrated (yes, it happens even to those of us who know better), I immediately began telling her that I had been a customer for years, had always paid our entire bill at the end of each month, anyone could see this was an inadvertent mistake on my part, and charging interest for the entire amount of the charges was not fair since I had paid all but $60. Twice the representative said, "What do you want me to do?" When I finally realized she was not being sarcastic or difficult but was trying to give me a message, I said, "I want you to remove the entire interest charged." Immediately she replied, "Okay, I'll be happy to do that.

I surmised from this experience that some companies will comply with *specific* requests from consumers, but their representatives are not allowed to offer or suggest solutions. This observation was confirmed recently when, although mailed well in advance, my payment did not reach my credit card company until a day or two after the due date. The company charged me a $39 late fee. I called and calmly told them

I had mailed payment a week in advance of the due date and asked that the charge be removed. My request was immediately honored. Later, when I sat down to pay our bill, I noticed that a finance charge of almost $12 had been added. This charge was located in the area that shows a total for deposits and withdrawals. I again called the company, this time to question the finance charge. I was told the charge was due to the late fee (talk about a double whammy). I asked them to remove this charge also. They agreed. With the total expenditure of five minutes of my time, I had saved over $50.

Of course there are times when companies simply do not want to listen to or honor our requests. Recently my husband and I faced yet another hard drive crash on the Dell laptop that I had bought new three years earlier. This was the third failed hard drive in three years. I'm sure you can imagine how happy that made me. Although the company sent a replacement hard drive after each crash and talked my husband through each installation, they did not seem to feel three failed hard drives in as many years was excessive.

I don't know about you, but I must disagree. To me this failure rate is totally unacceptable. Yet, in spite of my requests, Dell made it clear they were not willing to replace my computer. I couldn't detect much concern when I pointed out that these repeated hard drive failures wasted my time, my husband's time, and Dell's time. Nor did I make any progress when I explained how upsetting it was to lose data because, no matter how often I backed up my work, each crash invariably resulted in the loss of some data.

I stated repeatedly that while I knew I could not force Dell to behave in what I considered an honorable manner, I certainly did have control over my future purchases. I asked one of the representatives what he thought the chances were that Dan or I would buy another product from Dell. You're right, (and I'll bet he figured it out too), it will be way beyond when hell freezes over. One employee actually informed me that

Dell has little control over the problem because Dell doesn't manufacture hard drives and it is difficult to find a company that produces quality hard drives. If true, why is Dell still buying and installing inferior hard drives?

Not willing to give up, Dan and I continued to call and talk to numerous techs and consumer reps letting each one know we intended to share our experience with as many consumers as possible. Each time someone indicated he/she could not help other than to send us a new hard drive, we asked to speak to his/her supervisor. We assured each person that we had no interest in, or any intention of, installing a fourth hard drive, nor were we interested in staying on the phone while someone ran us through the same useless tests the techs had run us through so many times before. We continued to request a new computer.

After many persistent hours on the phone, Dell finally agreed to send me a new (i.e. refurbished) laptop. In fact they upgraded me to a newer, better model. I was certainly happy and grateful, though disappointed it had taken Dell so long to make things right. (Please see Lesson 14 for "the end of the story.")

As consumers we do have power and we need to exercise this power. Think for a minute. Do you want to do business with a company that has treated others unfairly? I don't. More and more people are turning to the internet to share their experiences. Several months ago, Dan and I read a long internet story having to do with the purchase of carpet from and installation by a large, well-known, major chain. The experience this couple described was so incredibly horrific that we decided against ordering windows from this company. Our decision will cost this company over $10,000. I plan to write to the company's home office and explain why we are not buying windows from them. We, as consumers, have tremendous power, but it does us no good unless we exercise this power.

As you have surely noted, the examples we have been discussing up to now have dealt primarily with consumer issues. However, the same principles apply equally well to friendships and other relationship issues. If someone is a true friend, he/she will be able to listen, discuss and resolve any issue that arises.

Years ago I met a young woman whom I enjoyed and admired. However, she had the disconcerting habit of picking her nose in public, and I mean, as she talked one-on-one to others and even in business meetings. Apparently no one had ever discussed this habit with her, although I knew for a fact that many others who interacted with her found this habit as revolting as I did. I realized I had two choices: avoid this young woman or talk with her about my reaction to her habit. Although it was not easy, I chose the latter option and approached this young woman in a private moment. She listened, thanked me for bringing this habit to her attention, and asked me to cue her if I ever saw her do it again. This was the beginning of a long and meaningful friendship that lasts to this day. How sad it would have been had

I chosen the *other* option. We both would have lost out on this meaningful friendship.

Dan and I have had several sets of friends who were consistently and significantly late when we invited them to dinner. We dearly loved all of these friends and eventually told each of them just how much their behavior frustrated us. Every one of them has made the effort to change this behavior.

My friend John is a quadriplegic. What a phenomenal man! Mutual acquaintances complained that John frequently smelled of urine thus was unpleasant to be around. However, they refused to talk to John about this problem saying they didn't want to hurt his feelings. Knowing John didn't need to be any more isolated than he already was, especially when the problem could be fixed so easily, I mentioned the odor problem to him. He was so grateful. John explained that medication had destroyed his sense of smell and because the urine bags were so expensive, he had tried to change them a few days later than recommended in order to save money. Being alerted to the problem, John corrected it immediately.

LESSON FOUR:
Actions Speak Louder Than Words

Although I typically advocate talking first, there are times when immediate action speaks more eloquently and convincingly. I smile as I think of our retired friend Warren who provides the following examples:

On crutches and equipped with a handicap sticker, Warren ventured forth to the store for the first time since his accident. Here he encountered a supplier of vending machines parked in the only remaining handicapped parking space. Did Warren park elsewhere and risk a difficult trek across the lot? No! Did Warren become upset, agitated, or allow this experience to ruin his day? No! Did he inconvenience himself by driving around until a handicap spot was vacant? No! Did he leave and return to the store at a later time? No! Warren simply parked his vehicle in tight behind the truck, effectively blocking its exit. He then proceeded into the store to do his shopping. Was the truck driver upset? Of course he was. That was the intent. We both hope this driver did not violate handicap parking again.

The street leading to Warren's house is five miles long with plenty of spaces for vehicles to pull over. Most of the school bus drivers will pull over every now and then to allow the cars behind them to pass since the school bus stops every tenth of a mile or so. On one occasion however, Warren was behind a bus driver who refused to pull over no matter how many cars were held up behind him. Warren lives at the very end of the road so his trip home was very slow and extremely irritating. Finally the bus came to its last stop and pulled into a side street to turn around. Warren pulled in behind the bus and sat there. There was no way the bus driver could turn around or return to the main street. Warren explained that he felt it was important for the bus driver to experience the same frustration that all those cars behind him had experienced. Hopefully this worked.

I recall a time when actions, of quite a different kind, spoke volumes, without words. Dan had to attend a conference on the east coast. At the time I was trying to teach myself Spanish in order to pass the language requirement for my Ph.D. program. Dan wanted me to accompany him, and I wanted to go. I decided I could study Spanish while Dan was in meetings.

The first morning, as soon as Dan left for the conference, I decided to take a shower, wash my hair and then settle down for a full day of study. Dan would call me when the meeting was over, I would grab a cab and meet him and friends for dinner.

Our room was large but the bathroom was tiny so the only thing I took in with me was a jar of face cream. Exiting the shower, I grabbed a towel and reached for the bathroom door. It would not open. The door opened inward so I could not throw my weight against it. Again and again I pulled. Nothing happened.

Although I have difficulty being in any confined space, I was determined not to succumb to panic. Ah, I would open the window in hopes of relieving my growing sense of confinement while at the same time giving the steam a quick avenue of escape. Surely the door would then open. I pushed on the window. It too was stuck!

Two hours later, the steam long gone and having tried repeatedly to open the door and window, I had to face facts. It would be hours and hours before anyone found me. Dan would not be returning to our room, no one would be calling (not that I could answer the phone anyway) and, to add insult to injury, I could not even study Spanish since all my materials were in the bedroom. This was the final straw. Climbing up on the toilet seat I looked through the unfrosted, top half of the window. Just across a delivery driveway, in another wing of the hotel, I could see several men gathered in a room; their windows were wide open. I knew I had to draw their attention.

From my perch, I looked down upon the only item in the bathroom -- my jar of cold cream. Reaching down impulsively (no panic here, right?), I grasped the jar and smashed it, and my fist, through the window. (Can you believe I didn't think to wrap my hand in a towel?) The men heard the glass break or perhaps it was the glass striking the driveway below that alerted them. However, looking out the window, I soon realized they could not see me; the sun was in their eyes. They started to close their window. Panic set in (as if I were not already panicked). All I could do was wail, "Don't close that window, please don't close your window."

Apparently a manager type, who was on the lower level accepting a delivery, heard me yelling, came out into the driveway, looked up, saw this half naked woman leaning out the window (the towel, not all that big to begin with, had slipped), heard my screams and called up to me in a huffy voice, "YOU, stop making all that noise, right now! Put on your clothes this minute!" I don't recall what else he said, but at that moment all my feelings of panic vanished and were replaced by cold fury. In a calm, if icy, voice (note: my voice was not bitchy, just firm), I informed him that I had been stuck in his tiny bathroom for over two hours, and if he did not have me out of there within three minutes he would have more than a broken window and naked woman to worry about.

The manager immediately turned solicitous asking what room I was in. Maintenance men rushed to the door. Unfortunately I had followed the request posted on the room door asking guests to secure the safety chain before showering or retiring for the night. The manager called to me from the hallway explaining he just needed a few more minutes as maintenance had to find bolt cutters. Finally the men returned and gained entry to my room. Knowing the hotel towels were rather small, and surmising (no doubt from the window encounter) that I had no clothes with me in the bathroom, the manager instructed me to stand back. The men would force the door and leave. Once dressed, I should meet him at the front desk. Reasonable? Yes. Did I follow instructions? No way! Two men forced the door and I was out of there like a shot. I didn't care what they saw, I just wanted space and freedom.

Minutes later (yes, with clothes on), I met with the manager. I just looked at him. I didn't need to say a word. He quickly explained that our room had been freshly painted; management had "thought" the paint was dry. Add steam, and the door and window were painted shut. He then told me he was moving us upstairs to a lovely suite. A fruit basket and wine awaited me. Our clothes and luggage would be transferred by staff. There would, of course, be no charge for the room.

LESSON FIVE:
You Can't Judge a Book by Its Cover

Living on an island, we often shop by catalog. Initially I was too busy deciding what to buy, especially from companies who advertised *free shipping,* to check shipping costs. It took me awhile before I learned to check the small print in each catalog.

Eventually I caught on and not only started reading the small print but began to listen carefully when placing an order. (WOW! The things I learned about shipping charges.) I learned that not all companies reveal their shipping charges. CONCLUSION: If they don't tell you, ask. I found that many companies were automatically adding a surcharge, often as high as $10 to $25, to orders outside the 48 contiguous states. And I found free shipping offers frequently do not apply to Hawaii and Alaska, interesting since a check with the post office convinced me the charge for shipping most packages from California to Hawaii was no greater than from California to New York. Even for those of you who live on the mainland, I suggest you pay attention to shipping charges. I believe you will be shocked.

I have learned to routinely ask about the shipping charges after I place an order. Yes, I said AFTER. When I find a surcharge is added or discover any other inequity, I immediately ask for a supervisor and nicely voice my displeasure. Sometimes the surcharge is removed. When it's not, what do I do? I cancel my order. Many people have asked me why I don't ask about shipping and other company practices before placing my order. To put it simply -- I want the order in place, I want the supervisor to know how much money the company is losing when I cancel my order, and I want to waste their time and resources just as they have wasted mine. Before hanging up, I insist our name be removed from their mailing list.

Can you imagine the potential effect on revenue if everyone stood firm and refused to pay surcharges or other discriminatory charges? Gosh, those of us who live in Hawaii might even convince some companies that Hawaii truly is part of the United States.

LESSON SIX:
Some Like It Hot!

How many times have you been seated in a restaurant eagerly anticipating a great meal when your food arrives cold, or undercooked, or overcooked, or you are not given what you ordered? You know what I'm talking about.

It never ceases to amaze me how few people are willing to send food back to the kitchen. When questioned, people have told me they do not wish to inconvenience the wait person, they do not want to call attention to themselves, that they can "make do." It does not seem to matter that this may be the only time they have eaten out in a month or that the meal is costing them a small fortune, often a small fortune which they can ill afford. Too many people consistently devalue themselves by settling for less than an excellent meal. It is as if they believe they do not have a right to expect exactly what they ordered and what they are paying for. When they take any action at all, it is usually in the form of making a decision never to return to that restaurant.

There are other responses that confuse me even more. What good does it do to become upset with the wait person when the kitchen is to blame or with the salesclerk when the problem is with the manufacturer? There is no need to humiliate, hassle or hurt others. Let me emphasize once again, TO BITCH DOES NOT GIVE US LICENSE TO BE BITCHY! It does not free us to make a scene. Kindness, sincerity, persistence and thoughtfulness go a long way in resolving any problem. Remember you don't need to be the noun to enact the verb.

I recall one night when my husband and I were eating with a group of friends in a nice restaurant. I had ordered a steak, rare, but when I cut into it, the steak was somewhere between medium and medium well. (YUCK!) I quietly told the waitress my steak was not as ordered, assured her I knew this was not her fault, and asked her to have another steak cooked for me. I also asked her to leave me the potato and veggies. This enabled me to continue to eat with my friends so they would not feel uncomfortable. The new steak arrived cooked to perfection. I ate about one third of it, then, as the others in our party had finished their meals, I took the remainder of my steak home. (Thoughtful? Not really. Mostly I was simply anxious to order one of their delicious desserts.) It provided us with great sandwiches the next day.

Some people have told me they are afraid to return food for fear of acts of revenge from the kitchen or wait staff. Usually if you "bitch" in a kind, caring way, this is not a problem. However,

Samantha Payne

if you have reason to believe the place where you are dining is capable of such dirty tricks, simply return the item in question, ask for a refund and do not accept a replacement.

All this talk of food makes me...yes, you guessed it, hungry. It makes me want to stop writing and go get something to eat. But I will show some self restraint here and write on. Fortunately all this talk of food also reminds me of an experience we had with Jessica when she was in her mid teens. Jessica wanted to order lobster at a restaurant. This was by far the most expensive meal on the menu. Dan and I were not particularly thrilled with her choice, but since we were on vacation, we told her to go ahead.

Our meals were served and eventually Dan and I noticed that Jessica seemed to be moving her lobster around and around her plate rather than eating it. We asked her if something was wrong. Jess told us her lobster did not taste right but had not wanted to complain since we had allowed her to order it. We sampled the lobster and found it spoiled. We called the waiter and asked him to remove the offending crustacean.

He did so and offered to bring Jessica another meal, but she was too sickened by her attempt to eat the lobster to want anything else. Therefore we asked him to remove the cost of her meal from our bill. The waiter said he could not do this.

Rather than argue with him, we asked to speak with the manager. We were very calm and courteous as we explained the problem. The manager immediately agreed to remove the charge for the lobster from our bill and treated us all to wonderful desserts. (Okay, okay, you are right. We did not **need** dessert, but after all, this was vacation and, far be it for me to risk hurting the manager's feelings by refusing his delicious offer.)

I realize this is lots of food talk so let me give you a non-food example. Umm. Oh dear, I can't think of one right now. Maybe later?

LESSON SEVEN:
Nothing Ventured,
Nothing Gained

Dan and I became acquainted with a college professor who was the victim of gender bias. Part way through the semester, she found she had twice as many classes, twice as many students in her classes and was being paid considerably less then her male counterparts.

While these issues were being investigated, this professor took a leave of absence and taught elsewhere. Eventually the issues were settled and back pay was received. However when it was time for her to return to the college that had treated her so unfairly, the professor found that she was becoming depressed and anxious. Ultimately she decided not to return at all even though this meant she would be jobless. She felt confused and angry and believed that the college owed her something for all they had put her through. With help she was able to set aside her anger and frustration and to use her energy to develop a plan. By this time the administration had changed. At our suggestion, this professor made an appointment to talk with the Dean. What was there to lose? The new Dean, understanding what the teacher had gone through and what she was feeling, agreed to and was able to deliver a generous severance package.

LESSON EIGHT:
Speak Softly but Carry a Big Stick

Too often when something goes wrong, people become upset, period! The tendency is to go over and over the offending act or problem either mentally (to oneself), or out loud (to others), or both. If a person confronts the situation at all, he or she often does it without thinking the situation through. Yet, it is the *solution*, not the offending act that needs to be thought about and mentally rehearsed.

Several years ago, our daughter and her girlfriend moved to the East Coast to attend graduate school. Being a Mom, (and all you mothers reading this book know what I mean), I went with them when they rented a truck from a well-known truck rental company. I explained my concern about two young women setting out on a 3000-mile trip from Nevada to Massachusetts. I was assured that the truck they were renting would be 100% road worthy. (I later learned when the girls picked up the truck, they were told to ignore any smoke. The rental agent said brakes frequently smoke from use when going over mountains. RIGHT!)

Jessica and Marla could write a book about this trip and what was wrong with that truck starting with a cab frequently filled with so much smoke they had to drive with the windows down. (So much for paying extra for air conditioning.) After the engine blew up in Pennsylvania, the girls learned that the truck had been due for its safety inspection less than half way to their destination and never should have been rented to them for their long trip. In addition, the mechanic who towed the truck told the girls the truck had two oil leaks, the tires were dangerously splayed, and the lights on the car dolly (which the rental company had hooked up for them) not only did not work properly but could not be fixed. The next day the girls were given a different truck. The intervening period had been replete with misinformation, false reassurances and promises by the much touted (but extremely unreliable) company hot line.

When the girls finally arrived in Massachusetts, they contacted the corporate office. They were told they would be reimbursed for the motel room and meals during the time they were awaiting a new truck, but the company was not willing to make any other settlement. When the girls persisted they were offered one hundred dollars, an offer that eventually was increased to three hundred-dollars. The girls refused. The company dug in their heels. This is when the girls called Bitch Incorporated -- better known as *Mom*.

The first step was to help the girls to stop focusing on their frustration and to decide exactly what they wanted from the rental company. Initially they considered accepting reimbursement for half of the rental expenses. I suggested they ask for more, not only to have negotiating room but also due to the principles involved. (I'm big on principles.)

I then wrote two separate letters to the rental company, one for the girls' signatures and another for mine. At no time did I mention filing a lawsuit. What I did, however, was to thoroughly document the entire incident. Words such as "lethal weapon," (referring to the truck), "criminal negligence," (referring to knowingly renting a truck scheduled for inspection and obviously not road worthy) and the mention of "possible lung damage" (the inhalation of all that smoke the girls were told to ignore) were, I must admit, designed to make the company worry about a lawsuit.

I also made a number of phone calls. When I could not get anyone from the home office to call me back, I called the people who rented the truck to the girls telling them I had no choice but to seek damages from them since the parent company would not return my calls. They ever so quickly convinced the home office to call me. As I was handed up the chain of command, I received numerous phone calls. I did not argue; I did not threaten. Having carefully thought about all the facts, and after looking at all the evidence, I felt comfortable with the solution I would be pitching to the company. This gave me a feeling of confidence and calmness. No matter what the various company representatives said, I kept repeating my conditions over and over again -- we want full reimbursement! Time and again I pointed out that we had a written report (note: this was our big stick) from the mechanic--their own chosen mechanic, I persistently pointed out. He had examined the truck after it broke down.

As the figure offered by the company moved upward, I eventually told them that, although I was against it (this was true, I would have held out for more) the girls would settle for reimbursement of that portion of the trip that had proved a nightmare, the trip from Nevada to Pennsylvania. The girls were willing to pay for the portion of the trip from Pennsylvania to Massachusetts since it was there they had finally received a reliable truck. The truck rental company eventually agreed. The girls were reimbursed for everything, including the numerous phone calls they had made to us back in Nevada. They paid only for the truck rental from Pennsylvania to Massachusetts. (And yes, I independently checked the company's rates from PA to MA.) My total time expenditure was under six hours!

None of this negotiation was the least bit stressful. In fact it was a good deal of fun, much like playing poker. Why did I feel so confident in the hand I was playing? Remember, I knew I had a pretty compelling big stick -- the report written by and obtained from the mechanic this company hired. But -- and this is very important -- having a big stick is not enough. The solution to the problem must be presented with calmness and persistence in a self-assured manner. Much like a weak poker hand, even a little stick can be compelling if you stay calm and persistent. Unlike poker, however, I would not recommend that you pretend to have a stick (data, evidence, proof -- whatever you want to call it), regardless of size, unless you actually have one.

I displayed no (obvious) anger that the company could hope would eventually cool. I made it clear I had no time limit and was in this for the long haul. I made sure they understood my main concern was the principle involved and that I was willing to spend any amount of money to make certain they took responsibility for their neglectful and dangerous actions. They did not know whether I had money or not, although to foster the impression that I did, I had initially introduced myself as Dr. Payne and referred to myself that way consistently throughout the negotiations. (As a psychologist in private practice I seldom used my title as I preferred that my clients call me Sam, but I knew that Ph.D. title would come in handy one day.) It is important to remember that part of thinking through facts and options is discovering and then using any and every tool possible.

Remember, the "big stick" is important, *but* the way you present yourself and your case is equally important. Before confronting a situation, take the time to figure out what leverage you have. Then make believers out of those you are dealing with by presenting your case with ease and confidence. Do not threaten, this will only backfire. You need to be confident in your position and calm in your presentation, regardless of what you are feeling inside.

LESSON NINE:
Resistance Meets Persistence

One rainy night, shortly after moving to Nevada, I headed to the grocery store. It had been a long day, and I really did not want to go out. Because of the rain, rather than follow my usual habit of parking as far as possible from the store entrance (love that exercise), I took a few minutes to hunt for parking close to the store. As I cruised the lane directly in front of the store, I saw someone backing out of a space. I flicked on my left blinker, preparing to turn into that aisle. Moments later, as I started my turn, a car accelerated and attempted to pass me on the left. Obviously, metal met metal.

I exited my car as did the driver of the vehicle that hit me. He tried to tell me I did not have my blinker on, but a witness pointed to my left turn signal which was still blinking. The same witness took me aside and told me the driver had been drinking a beer as he tried to pass me. (Umm, I wonder if this possibly could be the reason he failed to see my blinker?) The witness also told me that the driver and his passenger had hidden a six-pack of beer in a nearby grocery cart while I was in the store calling the police. Fortunately the police responded (it turns out they didn't have to respond as the parking lot was on private property), found the beer and cited the driver.

As I finally headed home, I believed I was merely a bit shaken, but during the night I awoke in pain and found I could hardly move. Eventually I went to a chiropractor. When I contacted the insurance company of the man who hit me, I found their employees' attitudes deplorable. I learned the company specialized in insuring high-risk drivers (for a very high premium of course). From the onset, not only were the company representatives unhelpful, but often they were downright hostile.

Had they been fair, I probably would have settled for expenses, but they seemed to think they could avoid responsibility through intimidation. (Wrong, wrong, wrong way to deal with people like me!) Rather than admitting that the young man they insured was high risk and had a disastrous driving record, they tried to make me feel the accident was somehow my fault and that they had no liability. As I said, WRONG APPROACH! This attitude was so pervasive among the company representatives that I couldn't help but wonder whether all of their employees were required to take a course entitled "Obnoxious Attitude 101."

Friends advised me to secure the services of an attorney. The attorney I talked with told me the most I could expect by way of settlement was three times my medical bills. Since my medical bills had totaled $1000, this would have amounted to $3000 ($1000 for the doctor, $1000 for the lawyer and $1000 for me). Earlier on this might have been okay, but by this time I was determined to personally teach a lesson to this company and its representatives. Principle loomed.

As I mentally stood back and watched the tactics of this company, I became more and more incredulous. I could not help but think about all the people they, undoubtedly, had intimidated into disappearing. I wanted them to pay, big time. I called them repeatedly. I used up as much of the representatives' time as I possibly could. I talked to them pointedly about my earnings as a psychologist and the income I would lose if I could not work. I was confident that eventually they would feel it best to settle with me. They asked me what I wanted. I told them $5000. They laughed and offered $1500. I calmly replied that I now wanted $5500. (I knew they would catch on eventually when they got around to really listening.)

I pointed out that they had chosen to insure high-risk clients and should expect to pay the consequences. I told them I had no idea how many more days I might miss from work since the doctor could not assure me that the condition would not reoccur. I also told them that I was having a difficult time understanding their attitude toward people who had been injured by THEIR HIGH RISK CLIENTS, and that I would not settle for less that $5500. I said all of this very nicely of course. (No, I am certainly not going to put into print what I was actually thinking.)

Each time a company representative offered less, I demanded more. Finally, they caught on (see, I told you they would catch on eventually) and we settled at $7500. However, I refused to accept the check they sent since they had subtracted the $1000 already paid to the doctor. After a few more go-rounds, they agreed to pay me $7500 *in addition* to what they had paid the doctor. I soon had their check in my hands.

LESSON TEN:
The Squeaky Wheel Gets the Oil

In rural Montana (is there any non rural part?) my friend Arlene had an interesting experience. The highway near her house was being resurfaced. As Arlene headed to work one day, she found her driveway blocked. The flag person told her she had to proceed along the drainage ditch and then up a steep embankment to reach the highway. When Arlene complied, her muffler was punctured. The replacement cost was $100 and she did not feel she should have to foot the bill. Arlene called the City; she was referred to the County, then to the Department of Transportation, then to one subcontractor after another. No one wanted to get involved; no one wanted to be responsible. Arlene would not let go. She made daily calls, sometimes several to the same person in one day. In other words, she continued to SQUEAK! She was determined. Finally, someone at the state level, realizing Arlene was not going to disappear without compensation, referred her to the contractor who hired the flag people. Although Arlene did have to fill out some forms and wait about five weeks, she eventually was reimbursed for her muffler.

Our daughter, Jessica had a problem with the screw-on antenna on her cell phone. Apparently it had been improperly installed, came off and was lost; without the antenna, reception was all but impossible – not acceptable when that's the only phone one has. Having owned the phone such a short time and never having touched the antenna, Jessica felt this was product design problem. She therefore called the company's customer service department only to be placed on hold, repeatedly. Several times she was cut off, and when she finally did get a real person, the representative said this was not their problem because they distribute, but do not manufacture, the phones. Jessica continued to call, sometimes reaching a real person, sometimes not.

Finally a company rep, after refusing to send Jessica a new antenna, did agree to send her a new phone - a much more expensive solution. Jessica was to return the old phone, but there would still be a considerable charge for this exchange. With the new phone on the way, Jessica recognized that she was not happy with this resolution. When the phone arrived Jessica decided, rather than reprogram her new phone, she would take the antenna from the new phone, put it on her old phone and return the new phone thus saving considerable time. She did this and returned the new phone minus the antenna.

More than fed up with the customer service department and not happy at the thought of paying anything for the antenna or phone, Jessica found a list of the various departments within the company. She called one that sounded promising. Here she reached a reasonable, sympathetic employee and explained to him all that had occurred. This kind man agreed with Jessica and told her the charge would be removed. Though frustrated by the amount of time it took to reach a satisfactory conclusion to this problem, Jessica, as a struggling graduate student, felt saving the money was worth the time spent.

LESSON ELEVEN:
Let Your Fingers
Do the Walking

When Arlene paid her telephone bill of $160, the bank removed this amount from her account but the telephone company made an encoding error and entered her payment as $1.60 rather than $160. They billed her with interest for the "balance." Arlene called the phone company to let them know about their error but they would not correct it. Each month the phone company religiously sent her a bill for the new amount complete with alleged interest owed.

Samantha Payne

Even though the bank issued paperwork showing the phone company they had been paid $160 not $1.06, and even though Arlene contacted the phone company repeatedly, they refused to make the correction. Interest continued to mount. Finally Arlene turned to the phone book to see who might be able to help. She decided to contact The Public Service Commission and after providing them with all documentation, the PSC contacted the phone company. This resulted in immediate action. The mistake was quickly corrected.

LESSON TWELVE:
The Pen is Mightier than the Sword

When my husband and I were first married, we lived on a very tight budget. I can't count the number of times one of us mentioned how wonderful it would be to have a freezer. We could then buy food when it was on sale. This was back when chuck roast, on sale, was twelve cents a pound -- yup, the olden days! More than anything, I wanted to surprise my husband with a freezer and I spent a year saving for one. Every extra cent I had, or could find (I literally picked up pennies when I saw them on the street) went into this fund. Money received from my parents for my birthday and Christmas went into this fund. Money I could shave from our already tight food budget went into this fund.

I made regular appearances at the appliance store a few miles down the street where they sold both new and used appliances. The store manager soon came to know me and to realize how determined I was to get my husband a freezer. Finally I had saved one hundred and twenty-five dollars. Thrilled, I returned to the store with a fist full of dollars! The manager showed me the three used freezers they had in stock, and although I liked the looks of one better than the other two, the manager urged me to buy the Norge saying, "It has a brand, new compressor and, after all, the compressor is everything!" I followed his advice, paid for the freezer and arranged to have it delivered the following month on my husband's birthday. In the meantime I was able to save a bit more money so we would be able to buy a little food for the freezer.

My husband was thrilled with his unexpected gift. That weekend, off we went to the grocery store. By the end of the month we had the freezer half filled with sale items and bread we had baked. We were content. We were content, that is, until the day we returned home to find a puddle of water around the freezer. The compressor was dead.

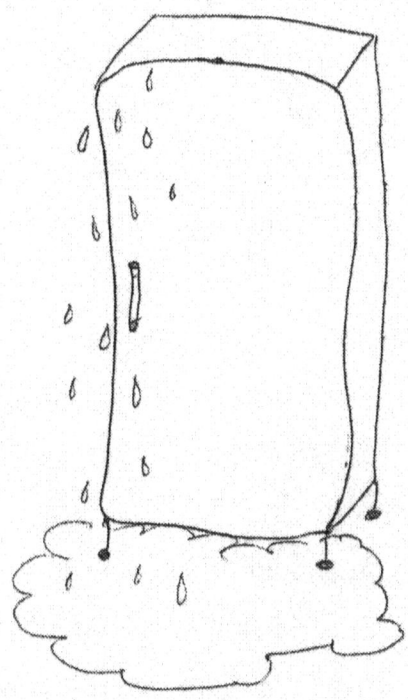

We had owned the freezer less than two months.

I was devastated and returned to the store. I knew, as a used appliance, the warranty was good for 30 days only, but I wanted to know how a "brand, new compressor" could die so quickly. I knew the manager would remember me and how hard I had worked to save for this freezer. He was the one who had pushed me to buy the Norge. Surely he would do something.

I talked calmly to the manager. He said he was sorry, but that there was nothing he could do. When I asked him about the "brand new" compressor, he said the compressor was new to the freezer but not a new, out-of-the-box compressor. In other words, he had misled (i.e. lied to) me. I pointed this out; he made no denial but did assure me there was nothing legally I could do about it. I pointed out that I felt he had a moral obligation. He smiled and said, "Sorry."

Saying goodbye, I walked away a few paces (okay, I plead guilty. I was setting him up, I admit it) and then turned back toward him with these questions. "Would you agree I have been calm about this situation?" He agreed. "Have I been polite and understanding as I listened to your explanation?" He nodded. I then continued, "Well, I hope you will be just as calm, polite and understanding when you discover what I am going to do." Once again I turned to walk away.

My statement grabbed his attention as I knew it would. The smug look left his face. He asked what I was talking about. I told him I was going across the street to the office supply store. There I would buy a large piece of heavy poster board and a marking pen. On that poster I would write the story of our freezer transaction, cover the poster with clear plastic to keep off the weather, attach it with wire to the back of my VW Bug, and park my car in front of his store. I assured him that I lived within walking distance of both college and my part time job so could survive without my car.

This was no idle threat. His store was in a small strip mall, so I was aware that I could easily park in front of his store. I also knew, if I were eventually blocked from using the parking lot, I could use the street equally well. The manager and I both knew that big signs attract big crowds. Human beings are curious by nature.

I ended by calmly saying, "Even though you don't feel you have a moral obligation to me, I do feel I have a moral obligation to your customers. I think people need to know what kind of businessman you are before they make purchases from you or this store." I then added sweetly, "You do understand, don't you?"

He understood all right! Within minutes this manager had agreed to have the freezer picked up from my home, to install a brand new, fresh out of the box, fully guaranteed compressor, and to return the freezer to my home -- all of this without charge.

Prior to going back to the store, I had decided if the manager was willing to meet me half way,

I would be satisfied. However, when I learned he had lied to me about the compressor, I decided to let others know of his business practices and had some misgivings about getting the new compressor rather than following through with my plan. Hopefully this man learned a much-needed lesson from our interaction. If he did not, and if he is still out there duping people, I hope you, at least, have learned something helpful. There are more businessmen like this one out there and you are bound to meet up with one of them; I want you to be ready.

LESSON THIRTEEN:
There's More than One Way to Skin a Cat

As mentioned before, many people believe that because they are only one person, or because they have to confront an entity bigger or more powerful than they are, there is no way they can win. Therefore they ask, "Why bother?"

There are all kinds of ways to win. Sometimes the only thing you can win is satisfaction, but what's wrong with that?

Shortly after our move to Hawaii, my husband and I made a quick stop at a major discount store. It was the Saturday before Christmas and, knowing the store would be crowded, we almost kept driving. After all, the only thing we needed was a plant pot. Still, we had to drive right by this store so ....

After parking the car we walked along the outside of the store toward the garden department. This meant passing the area where the Christmas trees were sold. Without warning, something hit me with such force that I went flying into my husband's side. A burning sensation seared my leg, the same leg that had been operated on earlier. At my feet was a large, heavy, wooden Christmas tree pallet. Apparently the pallet had been placed on its side and had somehow been jarred loose from its perilous perch. It was this that had come crashing into me. Blood dripped down my leg.

The two young men selling Christmas trees, who were responsible for the pallet's placement, did nothing and said nothing. We looked at them with amazement and still they did nothing. Entering the store, we spoke to a manager and filed the required report. We were told someone would contact us. The next day the manager did call; I told her that electric shock type sensations were passing intermittently through my leg. They arrived randomly without warning and lasted for varying lengths of time. I was also having pain in my back. The manager told me the store's insurance company would contact me. I waited until after the holidays and when they still had not called, I contacted them. The representative claimed she had called and not been able to reach me -- unbelievable since she had the correct number and we had an answering machine on which we had received many messages before, during and after the holidays.

The representative asked what I wanted. We discussed options and I told her I wanted to have 8-10 sessions of physical therapy on my back and leg. She indicated this sounded reasonable. To make a long story short, I was strung along for weeks with talks of meetings and pending decisions until finally the representative announced that since I had not sought help from a doctor in *all this time,* there must be nothing wrong with me. They offered me $100. I refused.

Now here's an interesting tidbit. One of the reasons I did not seek medical treatment immediately was due to the experience an acquaintance of mine had with this same national discount chain. My acquaintance was injured when a box of fireplace logs fell on her head while she was walking down an aisle; she suffered a concussion. Obviously, medical treatment could not be delayed. Yet, what did this particular discount store do? They refused payment to her saying her treatment had not been authorized and was probably unnecessary. It took several years but she took this company to court and won.

Notice the rules of this company's game. If you do not see a doctor right away, you must not be injured so *YOU LOSE.* If you do see a doctor on your own before getting authorization from the company, you didn't have permission so (you guessed it) *YOU LOSE.* Needless to say this company has developed quite a reputation for such shenanigans.

Since the treatment I needed was fairly minimal ($800-$1000), and would be covered in large part by my insurance company, I had no desire to take this company to court or involve myself in months, if not years, of legal wrangling. I knew I could derive much more pleasure and a far quicker "win" by boycotting this national chain instead. For almost two years, I avoided their store. At this time we were building and furnishing a new home and furnishing a vacation rental as well. I derived great pleasure in writing to this company and telling them of my one-man boycott, a boycott that cost them approximately $15,000 in sales. I also shared my experience and that of my acquaintance with other people whenever and wherever I had the opportunity. I know for a fact that at least some cut back on buying from this store. The $800-$1000 this company would have paid for my physical therapy, and the resulting good will, would have been money well spent for positive advertising. How un-insightful can some of these big companies be?

Now you may be thinking to yourself that a large discount chain would never miss my $15,000 and you may be right. But just imagine what would happen if the majority of consumers reacted the way I did. Think of the untapped power we, the consumers, have. Is it possible those big companies with their inflated sense of values and their dollar-sign eyes might finally begin to see the light? And please, please, please don't ever under-estimate the immense amount of satisfaction you can experience from a one-person boycott. In addition, you often gather important information. In my case, by avoiding this store, I discovered some wonderful, smaller, owner-managed stores where, though the prices are slightly higher, the service is outstanding. I still trade first in these stores. My sense of satisfaction is ongoing.

LESSON FOURTEEN:
To Bitch in Time Saves Mind

There are those of you out there (and you know who you are), who bitterly and continually complain when something goes wrong, yet take no action. There are others of you (and you know who you are), who will smile, make no complaint, try to convince yourselves it does not matter, and do nothing to correct the problem. And finally, there are those who blow up and then feel bad for having done so. There is considerable emotional cost for all of you and often for your friends and family members as well.

Peace of mind is important! How can this peaceful state be achieved when one is in internal or external turmoil? You know the answer -- peace of mind cannot be achieved under these circumstances.

The funny thing is, lodging a forthright complaint takes less time and energy than it requires to complain constantly to others (others being those who can't do anything about the problem), or to hold these feelings inside where they can continue to eat away at you.

It is certainly nice to voice a complaint and to reach an immediate and agreeable resolution. While this happens more often than people realize, none of us is so naïve as to believe this will happen each time. Peace of mind, however, can be achieved by recognizing that we have taken a stand, that the stand is justified, and that we have done our best to resolve the problem fairly.

Once we have done all we can, the best way we can, the issue should be put behind us. My

Samantha Payne

struggle with Dell, that you read about in Lesson 3, is a case in point. Approximately four months after receiving the newly refurbished computer from Dell to replace my constantly crashing laptop, I experienced yet another hard drive crash, this time with no slow down or warning of any kind. Experiencing the same problem with a second Dell computer, it no longer made sense for me to continue to deal with Dell. Peace of mind became my only goal and although I informed Dell of the problem, I told them I wanted nothing more to do with their company as I had zero faith in their product. No, I didn't want a new hard drive! No, I didn't want to take phone calls from their techs! I immediately ordered a new laptop, this time a Toshiba which, with its two large fans, seems to keep the computer (and hopefully the hard drive) cool. So far the Toshiba has been great and once again I have achieved peace of mind.

Years ago our family flew from Reno to Boston. Dan and I returned to Reno a week later. Jessica, age eleven, stayed behind to visit with her cousin in Maine for an additional week. She would then return to Reno via the same flights Dan and I took. This necessitated a plane change in Denver. When Dan and I checked in for our flight, we learned that a permanent change had been made in the connection time in Denver. Instead of a one and one half-hour layover in Denver, the time between the connecting flights had been changed to less than one hour. Our plane from Boston to Denver was delayed, and we were stuck in Denver overnight. While inconvenient, this was not an insurmountable problem for us. However we were very concerned at the thought of Jessica being stranded in Denver overnight.

As soon as we returned home, I called the airline. Explaining the potential problem caused by their change in connection time, I told them the age of our daughter and asked to have her changed to another flight. They refused. I asked to speak to a supervisor; the supervisor refused to change Jessica's flight. I asked what would happen to our daughter if she were stranded in

Denver like we were. The supervisor said the airline would either send Jessica home with one of the flight crew or put her in a hotel room with another passenger. As psychologists, Dan and I are all too aware of horrible acts perpetrated upon children and we said, "No way!"

After going round and round with various airline personnel, my mother volunteered to fly to Reno with Jessica. I attempted to buy my Mother a ticket on Jessica's flight only to be told the flight was full. Again airline personnel refused to switch our daughter to another flight. Refusing to give up, we finally located friends who were vacationing in the mountains of Colorado, a two-hour drive from Denver. They readily agreed that if Jessica missed her plane from Denver to Reno, they would drive down to Denver and get her. This was the best we could do.

On the day of departure, my sister, her husband, and Jessica's cousin drove to Boston to put Jessica on the plane. Once again they attempted to change her flight; once again the request was denied. Jessica's luggage was checked and the four of them proceeded to the boarding area. (Remember the days when this was possible?) After a long wait, boarding began along with the announcement (you'll love this) that the flight was overbooked. This was immediately followed by a request for Jessica and two other unaccompanied minors and their parents to come to the counter. Each was then informed that "it had been discovered" (oh what sleuths) that the time between landing in Denver and their respective continuation flights was too short! Therefore, the unaccompanied children would not be allowed on this flight but would have to be rebooked. The airlines had **suddenly discovered** a fact that Dan and I had been informing them of for a week. How interesting that their **discovery** allowed them to vacate three seats without having to pay three people to give up their seats on this flight. How very convenient!

Jessica was then rescheduled on another flight the following morning.

Samantha Payne

Letters were written to the airline by my parents, sister, brother-in-law, Dan and, of course, by me. We all received the same form letter apologizing for any problem that may have occurred and enclosing a $100 voucher to be used on our next flight with this airline. I tore mine into pieces and returned it to them with an additional letter informing them I would not fly their airline again nor would my parents, or any of my three sisters or their families. I also informed all of our friends of this episode. I know for a fact that I cost this particular airline a minimum of $25,000 in revenue. I'm sure they never knew, but I took great satisfaction in knowing this and in telling others of my boycott. I had done all I could; I had achieved peace of mind.

Footnote: In retrospect, I wish I had found a way to do more. During subsequent congressional hearings on airline treatment of passengers, one mother, according to a friend of mine, revealed that her six year old son, traveling as an unaccompanied minor, was put in a hotel room over night with a fifteen year old boy. During the hours that followed, her son was subjected to repeated sexual assault. Our fear became that family's nightmare.

LESSON FIFTEEN:
It's the Principle that Counts

In 1981 we moved from Virginia to Nevada. Several times, while still in the process of trying to fit furniture from our larger house into our much smaller rental, we had dinner at one of the casino buffets. On one of these occasions, as I swallowed the last bite of ham on my plate, something lodged deep within my throat. It felt like a piece of glass. After trying to dislodge the mystery object with various liquids and attempting to snare it with bread, I excused myself and hastened to the ladies room to attempt less refined extraction methods.   Nothing helped. Another restroom visitor, convinced I was about to expire, hastened to find a security guard.

The security guard insisted I go to the emergency room, assuring me the casino would pay for the visit. After waiting in the emergency room for what seemed like forever (many of you undoubtedly know all about these waits), I was seen by a family physician who happened to be at the hospital. I explained that 1) something was stuck in my throat, 2) it felt like glass, 3) at times it shifted positions, 4) it hurt like crazy. After examining my throat visually, the doctor asked for a laryngescope. He was told they did not have one available in the ER. After a whispered discussion with an ER doctor, most of which I overheard (lending yet one more proof to my husband's belief that I can hear anything and everything within a quarter mile radius), the family doctor came back to talk to me. He said that I was a very lucky girl, that nothing was lodged in my throat (yup, the same throat he couldn't see down into because the ER didn't have a laryngescope). He tried to convince me what I was feeling was a trace effect from being scratched by a hard piece of the ham's outer skin. His prescription -- go home, sip tea or other hot liquids. He insisted this would sooth my scratched throat as well as promote healing. I told him he was wrong and I left in disgust.

On the way home I could feel the object shifting position. It seemed to cut deeper into my throat and I was in enough pain that my husband decided to drive me into Reno (35 miles north) to the emergency room of another hospital. We first stopped by our house to pick up jackets and my husband insisted I take an aspirin to help with the pain. As the aspirin passed down my throat, it momentarily caught on the object already lodged therein. For a long moment I felt as if I could not breathe. Then both objects broke loose and I swallowed them. Fantastic! Within seconds the pain had disappeared except for a slight soreness. Hurrah, no trip to the Reno ER!

About a month later we received a bill from the family doctor who had seen me in the ER. I ignored it. When I received a second bill, I checked and found that the casino had paid for the ER doctor and all the ER expenses, but did not pay for the services of the family physician.

I wrote to the doctor explaining I was not willing to pay his bill. I recounted the entire episode, including what I had heard him say to the ER doctor, and reminded him how he had not wanted to wait around for the staff to locate a laryngescope. I explained that although the amount of his bill was relatively small, the principle involved was important to me. Therefore, I told him I would be more than willing to go to small claims court, tell my story to the judge (and everyone else in the court room) and let the judge decide whether I should pay. I might well have lost but not before numerous people in the courtroom heard the full story and judged this doctor's ethics for themselves. I never heard from this doctor again.

In a similar vein, just a few days before moving to Hawaii, we learned that my husband had a slightly elevated PSA. Of more concern to Dan's urologist was something the urologist could feel. He made Dan promise to see another doctor as soon as we arrived in Hawaii. Dan did go to an internist. The internist sent him to another doctor, a friend of his who was a urologist. Both of these doctors were convinced that what they, and Dan's mainland doctor, had felt was scar tissue buildup from a previous operation. The urologist did not believe a biopsy was necessary but said if we insisted on having one, the biopsy easily could wait until he (the urologist) returned from a lengthy trip outside of the US. This doctor repeatedly told Dan there was absolutely "no rush."

I had a bad feeling about waiting and, when I expressed my concern to the doctor, I was dismissed as an over-reactive wife. Although my husband tended to believe the doctor's finding was correct (and who wouldn't want to believe this), Dan, fortunately, has learned over the years not to discount my intuitive feelings. He therefore agreed to see another urologist. The new doctor quickly scheduled a biopsy, found cancer in both lobes and started treatment immediately.

Several months later when the first urologist finally arrived home from his extended vacation and sent us a bill, I sent him a note politely declining to pay. I gave him an update on Dan's medical tests and treatments and reminded him not only of the medical advice he had given us but of his attitude toward me. We never saw another bill.

LESSON SIXTEEN:
The Best Things in
Life are Free

(but best for whom? free for whom?)

Little has surprised me more than observing the numbers of people who cannot seem to bring themselves to say "no" to company. We first started hearing stories about uninvited guests when we moved to Nevada. (I guess some people figure why waste money on food and lodging when they can use all that money for gambling.) Since our move to Hawaii, we have heard even more "company" stories. I can understand having difficulty saying no to people you really like and would enjoy spending time with, but what shocked me was the difficulty some people have saying no to obvious freeloaders.

One woman told me how a couple she and her husband did not know and had never met, appeared on their doorstep with luggage in hand.

They apparently were friends of friends. This woman did not know how to turn them away and ended up housing and entertaining them for two weeks. Her reasoning: she did not want to offend their mutual friends. She was, however, very upset and exceedingly resentful.

In case you think such incidents are rare, let me assure you they are not. I have talked with a number of people who have told stories of friends who asked if friends of theirs could come to stay. I have also heard incredible stories of calls from mere acquaintances asking if they could come for a visit. In fact, just last week a friend called, frustrated and depressed, because she had learned that friends she and her husband thought were coming to stay with them a night or two while they were in Hawaii, were planning to spend all twelve nights of their vacation at their house. My friend and her husband like and enjoy these people but were not comfortable entertaining and feeding them for almost two weeks. Yet they did not tell these friends how they felt because they did not want to hurt their feelings. I'm willing to bet their friends picked up on these "hidden feelings" during their stay. What discomfort for all of them!

Other friends of ours bought two adjacent condos. They offered one of their condos to out-of-state friends for a two-week period expecting that their friends would rent their own car, entertain themselves, and eat out much of the time. Instead, these wealthy (wonder if this is how they became wealthy) people expected to be waited on, have every meal provided, entertainment planned, and to be chauffeured everywhere. After all, they were on vacation. Speechless, hurt, and angry, our friends (unfortunately) did all that was expected. Needless to say, the friendship ended with that visit.

Another woman told me a similar story. A friend of 20 years came to visit her here on the Big Island. Although my acquaintance was ill at the time, taking care of her daughter, and working hard at a new job, her visiting "friend" did nothing to help. She expected this woman to make her vacation a good one. Our acquaintance complied, but this experience ended their friendship.

I can't believe I am doing this. The book galley is ready for the printer and here I am adding more material. Why? Because this story fits too perfectly to be ignored. I just talked to a friend who sounded very down in the dumps when I called her. I asked her what was wrong. She told me and I am still shaking my head in disbelief.

I will call my friends Jane and Bill. Here is their story. Friends of theirs from the mainland called to say they wanted to come to Hawaii for vacation. Jane and her husband have a very small house with no room for company. Instead of directing these "friends" to a rental house or a hotel and getting together with them whenever it was mutually convenient, Jane agreed to find a house on the ocean for the four of them **and** to split the rental cost with these friends. The friends flew into an airport 110 miles from Jane's and Bill's home. Bill and Jane drove across the island, without complaint, to pick them up. The four of them stopped on their way home to shop for food and wine for the week. Guess who paid for everything? You're right, good old Jane and Bill. Guess who made both of their cars available throughout the vacation and paid for all the gas? Right again! Good old Jane and Bill. Their "friends" didn't pay for anything, but guess who complained all week long about everything from the weather to the accommodations to the activities proposed and/or provided? Not Bill and Jane. And when the guests had to spend the last night at Jane's and Bill's house, guess where Jane and Bill slept? Right again -- they gave their bedroom to their friends and they slept on the couch. Guess who complained anyway? Is this friendship? You be the judge. Incredible behavior on the part of these so-called friends? You bet! But what about Jane's and Bill's inability to stand up for themselves?

LESSON SEVENTEEN:
Honesty is the Best Policy

Situations such as those in the last lesson can easily be handled by taking two steps:

Step one: Ask yourself, "Do I want this person or these people as my guests?" If the answer is no, tell them so in plain, unequivocal terms, making certain your words are kind. If this ends the friendship, then it was not much of a friendship to begin with, so what have you lost?

If the answer is yes, you would like certain people to visit you, proceed to step two.

Step two: Give yourself plenty of time to think about their visit and to determine exactly what you feel willing and able to do with and for them. Then help your guests to understand your house rules BEFORE they arrive. This provides them plenty of time to decide if your terms are agreeable to them. They, of course, have the option of not coming or of staying elsewhere. If your "friends" are only willing to come for a visit when they can be fully housed, fed and entertained, this is information you need to have and to consider.

Recently a friend called asking if she could come for a visit in December or early January. She was having difficulty in her marriage and was dreading the holidays. I would have loved having her here, but because of problems in my extended family, I had to say no to my friend. She understood and said she was grateful for my candor. As events developed, this proved to be the best decision for both of us.

While living in Nevada, we received a call one day from people we barely knew. Jessica and the daughter had been classmates for a short time when they were six years old. Since the girls had lived miles apart, they had played together on rare occasions only. The parents announced they were traveling cross country, would be in Carson City within a day or two, and wanted to get together. Dan had the impression they hoped they could stay with us.

Since I was not home, Dan arranged for them to call back that evening. This gave Dan and me time to talk. Although we both agreed it would be interesting for Jessica and her classmate to reconnect after all these years, we did not feel it would work for us to have this family as overnight guests. While awaiting their call, I checked with various hotels and motels in the area and prepared a list of those with vacancies, but we did not hear from this family until about 7:30 the following evening when they called from a pay phone in town.

I explained we were busy that evening (which was true), read them the list of places with vacancies and suggested they come for a cookout the next afternoon. They agreed, but the next morning they called to say they had decided not to spend the previous night in Carson City. Instead they had driven to another town to visit friends and said they would call us on their way back through Carson City. Several days later they called and we invited them to join us for a cookout. The girls enjoyed seeing each other and we enjoyed chatting with the parents. Because we had offered what we felt we could, we were able to relax and truly enjoy the afternoon. They seemed to enjoy themselves as well.

Now, what about you? Let's say you receive a phone call, an e-mail or letter informing you that someone is planning to visit your area. This letter may contain a hint, outright request or even an announcement that this person intends or would like to stay with you. Please remember, no matter what they say or how they say it, it is your house and your decision.

Over the years Dan and I have developed a policy of always checking with one another before committing to a visit from anyone. We simply say, "Let me check with Dan (Sam) and I will get back to you." This approach prevents us from giving in to any sense of pressure. It also gives us time to discuss how each of us feels about the proposed visit and to decide whether the timing will work with our schedules. Often we are delighted at the thought of seeing guests and urge them to come for a visit, but on other occasions, as much as we may want to see someone, the timing simply will not work for us. And, of course, there are those requests where the timing is fine, but we don't particularly want to spend more than a day or two with someone who is suggesting or requesting a prolonged visit.

I remember well when Dan and I were first married. Both of us were enrolled in Ph.D. programs at the University of Colorado. I was in school full time and working part time; Dan was in school part time and working full time. Every minute was full. To make matters worse, Dan and I were both writing our specialty papers and studying for comprehensive exams when Dan's sister-in-law called to say she and Dan's brother were planning to spend their vacation with us in Colorado. Ordinarily we would have been thrilled to see them but the timing was horrible. Dan was caught unaware and simply did not know what to say. This sister-in-law had been very nice to him over the years and he hated to say "no." Of course, when Dan told me they were coming, I about had a stroke. We had never been busier or more stressed. Dan and I talked about the visit, the pros and cons, looked at it from every angle, and as much as we both wanted to see his relatives, we realized the timing was impossible. Even if they entertained themselves, they would be a distraction we could not afford at that time. Also, the guest bedroom was doubling as our much needed office. I was using it from 3:00 a.m. to 8:00 a.m. Dan was using it from 10:00 p.m. to 3:00 a.m. Reluctantly, we called back, explained the problem and asked Dan's relatives to come at another time. They were disappointed but did not disown us. They did come to see us during another vacation.

To reiterate, when Dan and I hear from someone who wants to come for a visit, the first thing we do is sit down together and ask ourselves, "Is this person someone we would like to have in our home for a few days? one week? two weeks?" If the answer is no, we simply write or call the person or persons, tell them that while we cannot have them as guests, (we offer no explanation) we would enjoy getting together for a few hours (a day, an evening, several times) while they are in our area. We offer to send them a list of reasonably priced rentals or hotels and suggest sights they might wish to see and places they might wish to visit while in the area.

Below is an excerpt from a letter I wrote shortly after we moved to Hawaii. A friend had repeatedly asked us when she and her boyfriend, whom we had never met, could visit us.

"Everyone who moves to Hawaii knows many people from the mainland and leaves behind many friends. Almost all of them would like to visit Hawaii. The result is that many of our Hawaii friends do little more with their lives than operate free hotels and act as tour guides. They are exhausted physically, emotionally and financially. We have watched many of our new friends struggle with a constant stream of company having no idea how to stem the flow. We have decided not to open the floodgates."

I went on to tell her that we were currently limiting our house guests to our immediate families (a big group in and of itself) but that we would love to see her and would certainly make plans to spend time with her if she decided to vacation here in Hawaii. She never came.

Even when we invite someone to stay with us, we remain aware of our own needs. We talk to our guests about our needs, and encourage them to think of their needs, when their trip is still in the planning stage. We let our guests know that they will need to rent their own car so they can do their own sightseeing. (We do, of course make exceptions to this condition but trust me, they are few.) We happily join our guests on some outings if they want us to, but we make it clear that they should not count on us as full time tour guides. We also describe our guest quarters. We have a small guest room with a queen-size bed. There is a sofa available in the adjoining den. They are welcome to either or both. We do not give up our bed (why should everyone sleep in a strange bed?); we do not make the twin bed in my office available since I arise between 3:00 and 4:00 each morning and proceed immediately to my office; we do not make the living room sofa available. We let guests know that they are more than welcome to eat with us any night they wish but that we do not plan elaborate meals. We tend to eat simple, mostly healthy meals (of course, we also have great, perhaps not so healthy, desserts) and do better when we stick to our regular eating habits. And yes, I expect guests to pitch in with clean up chores. This may be their vacation but our home is not a hotel and I am not a maid. So, if they don't offer to help (most do, of course), I am not shy about volunteering their services.

All the guests who have stayed in our home have been absolutely wonderful. To me the behavior and attitude of our guests is a clear signal of the kind of friendship we share. People who use and abuse your hospitality are not your friends!

As you read this, you may conclude that our conditions are downright unfriendly. Our guests, however, have repeatedly told us they find our approach to company refreshing. They know where we stand and where they stand. They arrive understanding our needs and expectations and are more comfortable knowing what to expect and what is expected of them. Our openness also encourages them to define their own needs and expectations and share those with us.

If you think back to your times as a guest in someone's home, you will probably realize that you needed time away from your hosts just as much as your hosts undoubtedly needed time away from you. Consider this: there is a major difference between guest and host. The guest is on vacation with few if any cares. In most cases the host is not on vacation; the host still has regular, on-going chores and responsibilities and must have time to take care of these. Guests are on vacation and need time to unwind and relax. They don't need someone talking to them full time. Everyone needs space. Arranging for it in advance benefits everyone.

As with any other type of situation where people cannot bring themselves to be direct and honest, much time can be wasted entertaining feelings of frustration, anger and entrapment. If you are willing to calmly think through the situation and to communicate your needs and feelings to your guests, well ahead of their arrival whenever possible, you will save much time and energy. In addition your friends will feel more relaxed around you. They will never have to worry about what you are *really thinking* or whether they are truly welcome in your home. You will already have given this information to them!

LESSON EIGHTEEN:
What's Good for the Goose is Good for the Gander

Not only should we strive to reach that point where we are able to comfortably stand up for ourselves, but we also must remember to be tolerant and understanding of others' rights to stand up for themselves.

For example, I remember the year, Tonia, my stepdaughter, returned two of the Christmas gifts we had given her. She explained, in a very kind way, that the onyx ring and earrings, though lovely, were "not her." Rather than pretend she liked them and then hide them in a drawer or pass them on to someone else, Tonia wanted to send them back to us so they could be returned to the store or given to someone else. The information she provided also helped us better understand Tonia's tastes.

It seems to be human nature to feel hurt, offended, disappointed and/or angry in a situation such as this. But think for a minute. How very refreshing! This is not an attack. In our case, we had given Tonia's gifts a good deal of thought but we simply missed the mark. Our mistake did not take away from our love, caring or intent. Tonia understood this. The returned gifts were not a rejection of us as people; Dan and I understood this. How wonderful that Tonia felt comfortable enough with us to trust us with her honest feelings. What more can one ask for in a relationship?

The important thing to remember is, as we learn to be honest, we need to be equally prepared to accept honesty from others. In fact,

Samantha Payne

we should encourage this kind of honesty for this is true friendship.

I recall another situation that was a bit touchy. Dan and I were invited to a friend's home for a gourmet dinner. John's gourmet group met once a month, each time at a different home. Knowing I was (I still am, YUM) a chocolate lover, John made a chocolate cheesecake in my honor. What he didn't know was that I had never tasted, nor do I ever plan to taste, cheesecake. I have so many edible vices that I decided, years ago, never to taste cheesecake. There is, of course, no doubt that I would love it. One bite and all would be lost and heaven knows I don't need more temptation! When I refused to try his chocolate cheesecake, John was hurt, but eventually he understood that I truly appreciated the thought and caring that went into the making of this dessert. This was what mattered. Of course, it didn't hurt that Dan and the gourmet club members loved that cheesecake right into oblivion.

LESSON NINETEEN:
You Can Catch More Flies with Honey

Prior to moving to Hawaii the health club in Nevada, where Dan and I exercised, was sold. We had been out of town for an extended period of time. When we returned, we were shocked by the steeply increased membership rates; we were also perplexed by the inflexible attitude with regard to part time residents.

We checked with other health clubs and found them not only more affordable but also more willing to meet our needs. Still, our preference was to continue working out at our old club. We

Samantha Payne

therefore returned to the club and asked to speak with the general manager. We discussed our need to have a half year membership since this particular club did not have a branch on the Big Island of Hawaii where we were spending several months each year. We showed him our quotes from other clubs for six-month memberships. We were honest about our desire to keep our membership at this club and praised the facility, layout, equipment and management. We did tell the manager, however, that if they could not meet our needs, we would understand but go elsewhere. The general manager worked out a special deal for us.

On another occasion Dan and I were stranded due to a cancelled flight. It was late, everyone was tired and many of the passengers were irate. Standing in a long line, Dan and I heard customer after customer berate the airline personnel who were trying their best to help each customer. We decided then and there that we would go out of our way to be kind and understanding when our turn came, regardless of outcome. Eventually we reached the counter. We immediately told the employee we knew she must be exhausted and that we were sorry some of the customers had given her such a difficult time. We even told a joke or two that started her laughing. After the employee had made the best alternate plans she could make for us, we thanked her and turned to go. She said, "Please, wait just a minute." She went into the back and came out with four $25 coupons and gave them to us.

During a trip to San Diego, we found that the timeshare we had been assigned was in a dark corner and the window looked out onto a wall. Timeshare rules said we could not ask for a change, but we decided to ask anyway. At the desk we calmly explained that we knew the rule and would understand if they could not or would not move us. We then explained that we had been looking forward to our vacation, found the assigned condo dark and depressing and would appreciate it if there was anything they could do for us. Telling us they were impressed with our attitude, they arranged to move us to another unit the next day.

More recently our daughter and a small group of students became stranded in London. They had flown in from Athens only to learn that their airline had gone on strike while they were in the air. Lines at every counter were huge and the wait to get to the counter was hours long. It was clear Jessica and her friends would not be able to talk to anyone at the counter until morning. Our daughter called us to see if we could do something by phone once the airport counters closed. When the counters closed in two hours, the hold that had been placed on all seats would be lifted.

The first agent I contacted was obviously frazzled and in a bad mood. She told me she could not get Jessica and the other students a flight to the US for at least five days. I was as nice as I knew how to be but nothing changed so I thanked her for trying and ended the call. Immediately I placed a second call, this time reaching a different agent. He too was exhausted. I told him how sorry I was to have to call and bother him when I knew he must have spent hours on the phone already. This agent responded positively to my genuine concern for him. He assured me he would find a way to get Jessica and her group home. Explaining that the strike only involved Heathrow Airport, he searched until he found seats for everyone the next day out of Gatwick. He even apologized when he could not get the entire group on the same flight.

The next morning, after sleeping on the airport floor to preserve their place in line, Jessica and her friends finally reached the counter. The agent looked at the computer screen and was shocked to discover Jessica and her friends already had reservations in the system. She told the group someone had done an outstanding job for them. The agent then issued the tickets and sent them to the shuttle, which would take them to Gatwick.

We find people are generally caring. They want to be helpful. It is important not to let our own frustrations and emotions set us up for failure. If we treat people with kindness and dignity, we often receive the same in return. And even when people don't reciprocate, we can feel good about our own behavior.

LESSON TWENTY:
When Honey Doesn't Work

During the years we lived in Virginia, my husband taught a statistics course at the community college. One student was having considerable difficulty, and Dan asked if I would please tutor this young man. The student was so grateful, he and his wife asked us to dinner in their home, and the wife and I became friendly. "Sarah" had no children, worked in a one-gal office and had lots of free time. My life was much busier and I had little time for or interest in talking on the phone. This upset Sarah who believed friends should talk daily.

Over a period of weeks I talked to Sarah many times, I listened to her expectations and concerns, and I tried to be understanding. Repeatedly, calmly and caringly I explained to Sarah, in every way I knew how, that I did not enjoy talking on the phone nor did I have time for long phone chats. I made sure she understood that my attitude had nothing to do with her, that I did not talk to anyone on the phone daily, that the amount of time I spent on the phone with someone had no relationship whatsoever to how much or little I cared for a person. My attempts to explain appeared to fall on deaf ears.

Sarah was alternately hurt, angry and upset. She would sulk, make unkind comments, or avoid me all together. Finally I had to end the relationship. I realized Sarah and I were never going to agree on the meaning of friendship, no compromise worked for long, and the friendship had simply become too much of a burden for me. I was sad but relieved when I reached my decision.

No one needs to be miserable, not me, not you, and not Sarah. Sarah had a right to have a friend who wanted to talk daily. I had a right to have a friend who didn't expect this. Neither of us was right. Neither of us was wrong. We were simply not a good match for each other. Again, what matters is willingness to work on issues. We need to give ourselves credit for trying. Remember, there is no such thing as one hundred percent success.

I have noted that some people seem to cope okay in situations where "honey doesn't work" **if** the people involved are not particularly close to them. In these situations they can simply decide not to buy a product, agree to disagree with an acquaintance, tune out an irritating office mate, terminate relationships that are not comfortable, or change jobs when a boss refuses to be reasonable. When it comes to family and close friends, however, many people act as if they have to put up with demanding or abusive behavior and/or stay in situations that violate their values.

We may wish to give family members and close friends extra consideration, but no one has the right to abuse us nor does it make sense for any of us to remain in a relationship that compromises our principles.

Several years ago a friend, after a year of anger and tears, finally stood her ground and lovingly explained to her husband that he had every right to continue drinking even though, from her point of view, alcohol was ruining his health, depleting their bank account, threatening his job and setting a horrible example for their children. She then made it clear that though she loved him, she also had the right to make her own decision. She resolved to take the children and leave if he chose to drink. He continued drinking. She left. A year later he entered a treatment program and three years later they reconciled.

An acquaintance took excellent care of his widowed mother but she was continually demanded more of him. In addition she frequently said mean and untrue things about him and his wife to others as well as to his face. He tired everything he could to improve their relationship but the situation continued to worsen. Eventually he calmly told his mother he would continue to take care of her financial needs but each time she lied about or was mean and hateful to him or his wife, he would not visit or call her for one week. At the end of the week they would try again. The next time she was hateful he would not see her for two weeks, then three weeks, then four weeks. What little improvement was made was very self-serving on his mother's part and eventually this man stopped seeing his mother completely.

Certainly our goal is to attempt to understand and resolve each problem that arises but we always have the right to stand up for ourselves, yes even (and perhaps especially) with those people who are closest to us. If, after honest and sincere effort the situation does not improve, we do not have to continue (and should not continue) in the situation, whatever that situation might be.

LESSON TWENTY-ONE:
The Proof is in the Pudding

When our daughter, Jessica, was five years old, she attended a Montessori school. Jessica loved her school but did not always follow the rules, for example the rule about never interrupting another child's lesson.

Jessica came home from school in tears one day saying her teacher had pushed her. Jessica insisted she was not going back to that school until I had talked to Ms. L and told her never to do that again. This kind of announcement often engenders one of two responses in a parent. Either the parent is ready to rush to the school in righteous indignation to confront or report the teacher or the parent immediately assumes the child was misbehaving and asks the child what he/she did wrong. Both responses can give inappropriate and harmful messages to the child. So, I put my arms around Jessica and asked her to tell me everything that had happened. Jessica told me she had interrupted another child's lesson to ask the teacher a question and the teacher had pushed her away quite forcefully.

As we talked calmly, Jessica volunteered that she knew she had done wrong by interrupting the lesson, but she pointed out that Ms. L "is all grown up and should know better than to push anyone, especially someone smaller like me." I agreed that they had both acted inappropriately and suggested that Jessica needed to go talk to her teacher. This definitely was not the response Jessica had hoped for. She wanted me to go to school and do the talking. I assured Jessica we can best learn by doing, and told her I would not consider having a talk with Ms. L until Jess talked

139

to her first. If things worked out well, there was no need for me to be involved. If things did not work out, then I would go with Jessica.

Far from impressed, Jessica felt unloved. She was upset with me. This attitude continued throughout the day and she was far from happy when I made her go to school the following morning. I explained that I could not make her talk to Ms. L, but she had to go to school.

Two days passed. On the third day I was working out in the yard waiting for Jessica's carpool to bring her home. When the car drove into the yard Jessica had her head out the window yelling, "Mom, I did it; I did it!" At first I had no clue as to her meaning, but by that time Jess was out of the car, running toward me yelling, "I talked with Ms. L and now we're friends."

We sat down, right there on the grass, while Jessica told me of their conversation. Jessica said she had reminded Ms. L how she had interrupted another child's lesson several days earlier and told Ms. L she was sorry for breaking the rule. She

then told Ms. L how surprised and hurt she was when Ms. L pushed her angrily away. Fortunately Ms. L admitted to Jessica that she too had been wrong and told Jessica she was sorry. Ms. L suggested each of them try harder to follow the rules. Then they hugged.

It was as if a giant burden had been lifted from Jessica's small shoulders, but perhaps more important, she was bursting with pride for resolving this problem on her own. Jessica felt

Samantha Payne

empowered -- a feeling that has lasted even to this day. Now a grown woman, Jessica has little problem confronting various situations whether they be interpersonal or consumer issues.

LESSON TWENTY-TWO:
David (or Davina)
Meets Goliath

Marla had a problem with the window controls on her Miata. She took her car to the dealership to be fixed and also had an oil change and tune up. The dealership told her there was no problem with the windows or wipers. As she drove away, Marla saw immediately that the window and wiper problem still existed. Back she went. A few days later her car overheated on the way to work--another trip to the dealership to have them again address the window and overheating problems. They "fixed it," Marla paid, and before she was back at work, the car overheated again. This time the dealership told her (in writing) that her car was not safe to drive, that it had all kinds of problems. Among other things they reported a cracked head and the need for new hoses and a new ignition switch. Marla refused all work except for the ignition switch. By this time the dealership had charged her over $400.

Marla then asked around and found a trustworthy, independent mechanic who went over her car thoroughly. Everything the dealership had told her was a lie -- there was no cracked head, no need for hoses. The mechanic easily fixed the window switch problem.

Marla returned to the dealership with the mechanic's written report. She confronted the manager and demanded her money back. He told her she would need to talk to his boss, the owner, who was not there. She asked the whereabouts of the owner and was told he was at one of the other car dealerships he owned. Marla said, "Fine, let's go!" and made it very clear she was not leaving without getting her money back, NOW!

They walked over to the other dealership. Marla showed the owner her paperwork. He knew she had the proof to hang them and said he would send her a check. She replied, "No, I am NOT leaving here without a total refund." Right then he had the accounting office cut a check for Marla, not only for all the money she had paid them but for the money she had paid the other mechanic for fixing her window switch.

We never know when we will need to stand up for ourselves, or over what issue or in what way. Sometime we have to confront a powerful and wealthy adversary. This can make the situation seem even more scary but the approach remains the same.

Last year, Dan and I had no option but to file our very first law suit. Five years ago we built a house on the ocean here on the Big Island of Hawaii. This was something we never thought we could afford to do; it was our dream come true. Since a synthetic stucco product had been used successfully on the exterior of the 7-year-old house next door, earning rave reviews from the owner, we decided to follow suit. Unfortunately, within a year our house was known as *The House of Measles and Mange*.

Bubbles of various sizes began to form on the overhangs, some larger than basketballs. Within hours to days, these bubbles would burst open and the color-coat layer would peel away and fall to the ground in shattered pieces. What a mess! Several experts told us it appeared the contractor who applied the material did not properly clean the salt spray off the prepared surface. Thus a good adhesion was not achieved.

To add insult to injury, the entire surface of our house developed rust spots, thousands of rust spots. And, although they came in several different colors of reds, oranges and browns, trust me, they were definitely not pretty! When the company who manufactured the synthetic stucco denied any blame, we had their product tested. Ferrous metal (as well as other metals) were found. The assumption was they were in the sand aggregate used by the company.

Since neither the contractor who applied the stucco nor the company who made the product was willing to work with us toward an acceptable solution, we finally consulted and hired an attorney and eventually went to mediation. Initially low offers of settlement were made. We refused them, AND increased the amount we had been asking for. (Does this sound familiar?). The contractor who applied the synthetic stucco caught on more quickly than the manufacturer of the product and settled first. Eventually we reached a satisfactory settlement with the manufacturer as well, an amount higher than we would have initially settled for had the defendant been cooperative from the start. Law suits and mediation are not for the faint hearted, but they are often worthwhile. If you have a solid case, a clear plan of approach and an able lawyer, you will likely do okay, but be prepared to do your own investigative work. Don't expect to sit back and let your attorney do it all. No one can be as interested in your case as you are, and no one will ever know the facts or remember the details as well as you do.

LESSON TWENTY-THREE:
Know when to Hold'em, Know when to Fold'em

The time has come for me to end this little book. By now I am sure you understand the point. There is no need for me to belabor it. Please remember, you do not have to be a victim -- not the victim of others or a victim of your own responses. You do have the power to stand up for yourself, to stand up for yourself appropriately, to bitch without being bitchy. If you stay calm and think things through, you can be just as creative as the next person in finding a solution to each and every problem. Never issue empty threats.

Determine what data you have and use it wisely. Go back and study the vignettes you have just read. Think of similar episodes from your own life. Replay them in your mind. Think of ways you can improve your responses when you find yourself in these kinds of situations in the future. Decide what feels best to you. You can practice anywhere, any time. As you practice you will continue to improve and grow. Good Luck. Who knows, maybe one day you will become so proficient in standing up for yourself that you will decide to open your own business and call it *Bitch Incorporated*.

About the Author

Dr Samantha Payne received her Ph.D. in psychology from the University of Colorado in 1973. She later did post graduate work at Virginia Commonwealth University, Richmond, Virginia and at the University of Nevada, Reno.

As far back as her early teens, Dr. Payne noted the large number of adults as well as peers who either stood up for themselves inappropriately or did not stand up for themselves at all. At seventeen she seriously considered opening a business called BITCH INCORPORATED, hiring out to do other peoples bitching for them while, at the same time, demonstrating how to bitch appropriately.

Throughout undergraduate and graduate school, and during her many years working as a psychologist, Dr. Payne continued to observe the same, disturbing pattern. Finding that many of her clients did not know how to stand up for themselves appropriately was not surprising. These folks were in therapy because they needed and wanted help. However, observing the same problem among friends, acquaintances and co-workers, of all ages and both sexes, in the general population was of grave concern. Many of them did not comprehend the extent to which their inability to stand up for themselves appropriately was playing havoc with their lives. Those who did had no idea how to solve this problem.

When she retired, Dr. Payne was determined to write a book about this problem, a book that would be applicable to women, men and teens, a book that would be fun to read and hopefully would make learning easy. ***BITCH INCORPORATED: How to Bitch Appropriately Without Being Bitchy*** is this book. Dr. Payne currently lives on the Big Island of Hawaii with her husband of 36 years.

www.ingramcontent.com/pod-product-compliance
Lightning Source LLC
Chambersburg PA
CBHW032018170526
45157CB00002B/757